Pebble® Plus

•HOLIDAY HISTORIES•

A Short History of

VALENTINE'S DAY

by Sally Lee

Consulting Editor: Gail Saunders-Smith, PhD
Consultant: Jeannine Diddle Uzzi, PhD,
Director of Faculty Programs,
Associated Colleges of the South

CAPSTONE PRESS
a capstone imprint

Pebble Plus is published by Capstone Press,
1710 Roe Crest Drive, North Mankato, Minnesota 56003
www.capstonepub.com

Library of Congress Cataloging-in-Publication Data
Lee, Sally.
  A short history of Valentine's Day / by Sally Lee.
    pages cm.—(Pebble plus. Holiday histories)
  Includes bibliographical references and index.
  ISBN 978-1-4914-6098-6 (library binding)—ISBN 978-1-4914-6102-0 (pbk.)
ISBN 978-1-4914-6106-8 (ebook pdf)
1. Valentine's Day—Juvenile literature. I. Title.
  GT4925.L4 2016
  394.2618—dc23   2015002031

Editorial Credits
Erika L. Shores, editor; Bobbie Nuytten, designer; Kelly Garvin, media researcher;
Karina Rose, production specialist

Photo Credits
Alamy/Niday Picture Library, 18; Courtesy, American Antiquarian Society, 17 (top right); Corbis/Bettmann, 19; iStockphoto/kirin_photo, 21; North Wind Picture Archives, 9, 15; Shutterstock: Dragon Images, 5, Garry L., 11, Kudryashka, cover (hearts), Symbiot, cover, Zvonimir Atletic, 7; Superstock/Buyenlarge, 13; Wikimedia/Mount Holyoke College Archives and Special Collections, 17 (left)

Design elements: Shutterstock/ankudi

Note to Parents and Teachers

The Holiday Histories set supports national curriculum standards for social studies. This book describes and illustrates the holiday of Valentine's Day. The images support early readers in understanding the text. The repetition of words and phrases helps early readers learn new words. This book also introduces early readers to subject-specific vocabulary words, which are defined in the Glossary section. Early readers may need assistance to read some words and to use the Table of Contents, Glossary, Read More, Internet Sites, Critical Thinking Using the Common Core, and Index sections of the book.

Printed in the United States of America in North Mankato, Minnesota.
042015   008823CGF15

Table of Contents

Hearts and Cards

Today is February 14.

It's Valentine's Day!

We see paper hearts. We give

cards to friends. Let's learn

the story behind this fun day.

Saint Valentine

Nobody knows for sure
how Valentine's Day started.
Many people believe
the holiday honors a priest
named Valentine.

7

Valentine lived in Rome, Italy.
One story about Valentine says
he married soldiers in secret.
At the time, the ruler of Rome
refused to let soldiers marry.

Another story says Valentine was killed for being a Christian. He died February 14 around 270. Later the Catholic Church decided to honor Saint Valentine on February 14.

A Loving Holiday

In the 1300s people began thinking of love on Valentine's Day. Poems told of birds finding mates around February 14. Birds became a symbol of love and Valentine's Day.

Making Valentines

England had the first valentine cards in the 1400s. People made them by hand. Then in the 1700s people also began to give flowers and candy on Valentine's Day.

Around 1847 Esther Howland started the first valentine card business in the United States. The handmade cards were sold in stores.

Later machines printed valentines.

Greeting card companies made

millions of valentines cheaply.

People everywhere gave cards

to loved ones.

A Special Day

Valentine's Day is a time

for cards, parties, and flowers.

But mostly it is a day to show

people we care about them.

Glossary

Christian—a person who follows the teachings of Jesus Christ

mate—the male or female partner of a pair of animals

poem—a piece of writing set out in short lines, often using some words that rhyme

saint—a very holy person

symbol—an object that reminds people of something else

priest—a person who has the right to lead services in some churches

Read More

McGee, Randel. *Paper Crafts for Valentine's Day.* Paper Craft Fun for Holidays. Berkeley Heights, N.J.: Enslow, 2013.

Trueit, Trudi Strain. *Valentine's Day.* Rookie Read-About Holidays. New York: Children's Press, 2013.

Internet Sites

FactHound offers a safe, fun way to find Internet sites related to this book. All of the sites on FactHound have been researched by our staff.

Here's all you do:

Visit *www.facthound.com*

Type in this code: 9781491460986

Super-cool stuff!

Check out projects, games and lots more at
www.capstonekids.com

Critical Thinking
Using the Common Core

1. Why are birds a symbol of Valentine's Day? (Key Ideas and Details)

2. Look at the photograph on page 19. Name some of the Valentine's Day symbols you see. (Craft and Structure)

Index

Word Count: 218
Grade: 1
Early-Intervention Level: 18